Mohandas Gandhi

A LIFE OF INTEGRITY

by Sheila Rivera

Lerner Publications Company • Minneapolis

Photo Acknowledgments

The photographs in this book are reproduced with the courtesy of: © Betmann/CORBIS, cover, pp. 22, 23; © Dinodia Photo Library, pp. 4, 15, 16, 18, 19, 26, 27; © Dinodia/The Image Works, pp. 6, 14; © Hulton-Deutsch Collection/CORBIS, pp. 7, 10, 20; © Stapleton Collection/CORBIS, p. 8; © E.O. Hoppe/CORBIS, p. 11; © Lindsay Hebberd/CORBIS, p. 12; © Bradley Smith/CORBIS, p. 13; © Mary Evans Picture Library, p. 24.

Text copyright © 2007 by Lerner Publications Company

Lerner Publications Company
A division of Lerner Publishing Group
241 First Avenue North
Minneapolis, MN 55401 U.S.A.

Website address: www.lernerbooks.com

Words in **bold type** are explained in a glossary on page 31.

Library of Congress Cataloging-in-Publication Data

Rivera, Sheila, 1970–
     Mohandas Gandhi : a life of integrity / by Sheila Rivera.
         p.   cm. – (Pull ahead books)
     Includes index.
     ISBN-13: 978–0–8225–6383–9 (lib. bdg. : alk. paper)
     ISBN-10: 0–8225–6383–5 (lib. bdg. : alk. paper)
     1. Gandhi, Mahatma, 1869–1948–Juvenile literature. 2. Statesmen–India–Biography–
Juvenile literature. 3. Nationalists–India–Biography–Juvenile literature. I. Title. II. Series.
DS481.G3R53 2007
954.03'5092–dc22   2005037923

Manufactured in the United States of America
1 2 3 4 5 6 – JR – 12 11 10 09 08 07

Table of Contents

Gandhi and his granddaughters

Who Was Mohandas Gandhi?

Mohandas Gandhi was a person with **integrity.** He was good, honest, and fair. Gandhi believed that all people should be treated fairly. They should be peaceful. They should accept people who are different than themselves. And he felt that his country should rule itself.

Mohandas Gandhi was born in India in 1869.

Gandhi, age 7

The British king visits India.

India was ruled by a country called Britain. Gandhi believed India should be free.

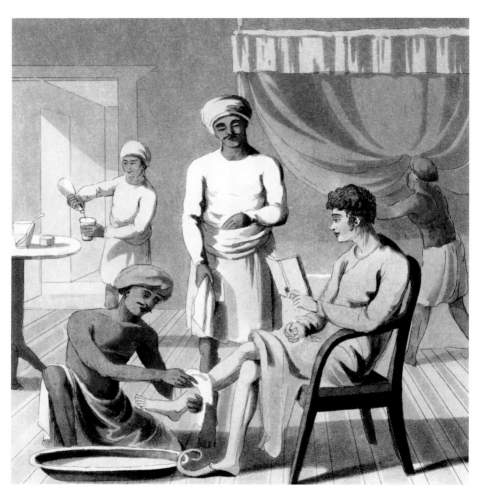

Indian servants wash a British woman's feet.

Unfair Treatment

British people in India did not treat Indians as equals. They would not be friends with Indians. They would not live in neighborhoods with Indians. Many Indians worked as servants for the British.

Indians did not treat each other as equals either. They were divided into groups. People in higher groups had more **rights** than people in lower groups.

People in the highest group wore nice clothes.

Untouchables did not have much money.

Indians in the lowest group were called **untouchables.**

Untouchables clean the street.

Untouchables did the jobs that no one else wanted to do. They were not paid much for their work.

People from other groups would not be friends with untouchables. Gandhi knew that it was wrong to treat people this way.

Untouchables tell a government worker that they need food.

Gandhi went to work in South Africa. This country was also ruled by Britain. He learned that Indians were treated poorly there too.

Gandhi in South Africa

Gandhi speaks to a police officer about poor working conditions.

Gandhi decided to stand up against the unfair way that Indians were treated. He would **protest** in a peaceful way.

16

Making a Difference

At this time, Indians and people of color did not have the same rights as white South Africans. People who were not white had to take their hats off when they met white people. Gandhi wore a **turban** on his head. He was told to take it off. But Gandhi did not take it off.

These Indians are marching against unfair laws.

Gandhi spoke about the unfair treatment of Indians. He and other Indians decided not to **obey** unfair laws.

People who broke the laws were sent to jail. Soon the jails were full. The South African government decided to change some of its unfair laws.

Gandhi writes in his jail cell.

A crowd gathers around Gandhi.

Mahatma

Gandhi returned to India in 1915. Nearly everyone in South Africa and India knew about him. People respected Gandhi for his integrity. They gave him the title **Mahatma.** This means "great soul."

These women broke the law by making their own salt.

In India, Indians were not allowed to make their own salt. They had to buy it from the British. Indians did not think this was fair.

Gandhi led people on a **march** to the sea. They gathered seawater and made their own salt. They did this to protest. They would not be treated unfairly.

Indians gather salt from the sea.

Gandhi refused to eat.

Freedom for All!

Gandhi was still upset about how untouchables were treated. He said he would not eat until people agreed to treat them like everyone else.

People thought Gandhi might die if he didn't eat. They agreed to treat untouchables the same as other Indians.

Gandhi meets with a group of untouchables.

Children celebrate Independence Day in India.

Gandhi continued to protest British control of India. Then, in 1947, Britain said India could rule itself. Gandhi's integrity helped India become free.

Mohandas Gandhi Timeline

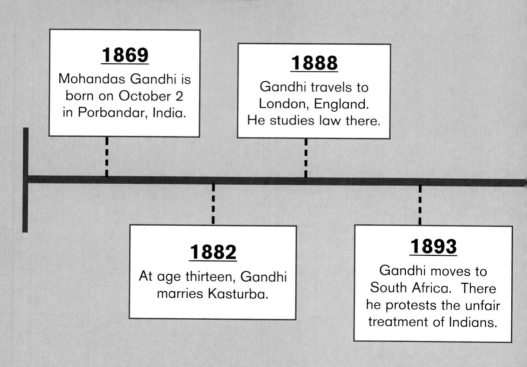

1869
Mohandas Gandhi is born on October 2 in Porbandar, India.

1888
Gandhi travels to London, England. He studies law there.

1882
At age thirteen, Gandhi marries Kasturba.

1893
Gandhi moves to South Africa. There he protests the unfair treatment of Indians.

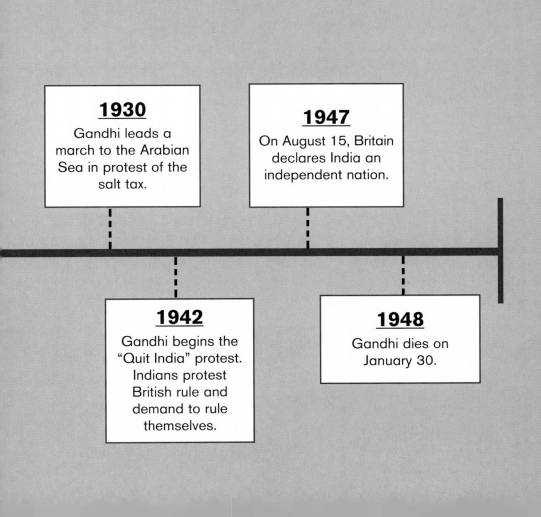

1930
Gandhi leads a march to the Arabian Sea in protest of the salt tax.

1947
On August 15, Britain declares India an independent nation.

1942
Gandhi begins the "Quit India" protest. Indians protest British rule and demand to rule themselves.

1948
Gandhi dies on January 30.

More about Mohandas Gandhi

● Gandhi wove thread for one hour each day. He encouraged Indians to make their own cloth instead of buying it from the British.

● Gandhi was a role model for Martin Luther King Jr. King was a leader in the U.S. civil rights movement in the 1960s.

● Gandhi was nominated for the Nobel Peace Prize five times for his work toward equal rights for all Indians.

Websites

The Complete Site on Mahatma Gandhi
http://www.mkgandhi.org/

Mahatma.com
http://www.mahatma.com/

Mahatma Gandhi Album
http://www.kamat.com/mmgandhi/

Glossary

integrity: to be good, honest, and fair; to hold firmly to one's beliefs

Mahatma: a title meaning "great soul"

march: people walking together for a purpose

obey: to carry out or do what is requested

protest: to express strong disagreement

rights: the power to do something

turban: a long cloth wound around a person's head

untouchables: people in the lowest group of the Indian social system

Index